D1458842

DESERTS

BY
MIKE CLARK

©2017
Book Life
King's Lynn
Norfolk PE30 4LS

Written by:
Mike Clark

ISBN: 978-1-78637-183-6

Edited by:
Charlie Ogden

Designed by:
Drue Rintoul

All rights reserved
Printed in Malaysia

A catalogue record for this book
is available from the British Library.

Photocredits
Abbreviations: l-left, r-right, b-bottom, t-top, c-centre, m-middle.

Front Cover Main – Ilyshev Dmitry. FCTL – Scisetti Alfio. FCTR – Videowokart. 1 – wacpan. 2 – Marques. 4tr – By Bob Palin (picture taken by Bob Palin with a Canon S70.) [CC BY-SA 2.5 (http://creativecommons.org/licenses/by-sa/2.5)], via Wikimedia Commons. 4bl – ThamKC. 5 – kenkistler. 6tr – apdesign. 7t – Ivan Hoermann. 8t – Jon Manjeot. 8b – Ekaterina Pokrovsky. 9tr – nuu_jeed. 9tl – AndreAnita. 9b – Yegor Larin. 10tr – angelo lano. 10b – Robert Szymanski. 11tr – arka38. 11b – Dmitry Sheremeta. 12tr – PK289. 12l – alfotokunst. 12br – Pavel Krasensky. 12b – Simone Caltabiano. 13tr – photopixel. 13l – By Tarantula_hawk.JPG: Astrobradley derivative work: B kimmel (Tarantula_hawk.JPG) [Public domain], via Wikimedia Commons. 13br – Protasov AN. 14l – EcoPrint. 14br – Tobie Oosthuizen. 15t – Tom Tietz. 15b – Sergey Uryadnikov. 16tr – Konrad Mostert. 16bl – Sarunyu_foto. 16br – Chris Fourie. 17t – RHIMAGE. 17br – PISHEVroman. 17bl – Bandurka. 18tr – withGod. 18b – Matt Jeppson. 19tl – Sheila Hammer. 19r – Eric Isselee. 19bl – Mari Swanepoel. 20tr – Andrey N Bannov. 20tl – © Hans Hillewaert / , via Wikimedia Commons. 20b – Eniko Balogh. 21t – pixy. 21cl – Pete Gallop. 21b – Maxim Petrichuk. 22tr – Tischenko Irina. 22b – photosounds. 23t – John Blanton. 23b – Yegor Larin. 24l - An Wenhong. 24c – ixpert. 25t – Erwin Niemand. 25br – S.Z.. 26bl – river34. 26c – ixpert. 27t – vladsilver. 27b – AJP. 27t – vladsilver. 27b – AJP. 28m – wrangler. 9t – amenic181. 29b – Jacek Chabraszewski. Images are courtesy of Shutterstock.com. With thanks to Getty Images, Thinkstock Photo and iStockphoto.

CONTENTS

Words in **bold** are explained in the glossary on page 31.

Habitats and Biomes

WHAT ARE HABITATS?

Habitats are places where plants and animals live. Habitats can include everything from mountains and rivers to deserts and oceans – even other living things!

The animals and plants that live in a habitat usually become **adapted** to it. This means that they become very good at raising their young and finding food and water in their specific habitat. A habitat can also keep the animal safe from **predators**, often by having lots of places to hide. This helps animals to **reproduce** safely.

The cliff swallow builds its nest high up on cliffs. Up here, it is safe from predators that cannot climb up the steep cliff face.

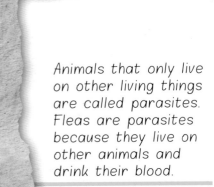

Animals that only live on other living things are called parasites. Fleas are parasites because they live on other animals and drink their blood.

WHAT IS A BIOME?

A biome is a very large area of the world where the **climate** is very similar. Because biomes are so huge, they usually contain many different habitats. As a biome's climate is the same all the way across it, many of the animals and plants that live in the same biome will adapt similar **traits**, even if they live in very different habitats. While some animals and plants are able to live in different habitats within the same biome, most living things can only live in one habitat.

For example, cactus plants can survive in dry deserts because they can store water. This helps them to survive long periods without rain. But in the rainforest, the cactus would not survive. Other plants would grow over the top of the cactus, blocking out the sunlight that the cactus needs to survive.

*Some plants survive better in the dry, sunny conditions of the desert, whereas other plants survive better in the dark, damp conditions of the rainforest. This shows how living things adapt to their **environment**.*

What Is a Desert?

A desert is a biome that gets very little rain. Most deserts are either very hot or very cold.

There are two main types of desert; hot deserts and cold deserts. Deserts get, at most, 25 centimetres of rainfall a year – a country like England expects to get about 80 centimetres a year. Deserts can be very difficult places to live in because both plants and animals need water to survive.

Sunshine causes water to **evaporate**. Evaporated water, which is known as water vapour, eventually forms into clouds. However, when the weather is too hot, the water vapour cannot cool and fall to the ground as rain. Hot deserts receive so much sunshine that it is very difficult for rainclouds to form. Cold deserts, on the other hand, have the opposite problem. There is not enough sunshine in these deserts for water to evaporate in the first place. The lack of sunshine also makes these deserts very cold, meaning that water often falls as snow instead of rain.

Hot Desert

Chihuahuan Desert
Type of Desert: Hot
Size: 362,600 km²

Hot deserts are the most common type of desert. These are mostly found near to or on the Equator. This is because the Equator is the part of the planet that gets the most sunshine. The largest hot desert in the world is the Sahara in Africa.

Cold deserts can only form in areas of the world that are very cold, such as around the North and South Poles, or in places that are very high above **sea level**. The largest cold desert in the world is Antarctica.

Cold Desert

Animal habitats in both hot and cold deserts are changing due to **global warming**. This is making it harder for some animals to survive.

Arabian Desert
Type of Desert: Hot
Size: 2.33 million km²

Sahara
Type of Desert: Hot
Size: 9.4 million km²

Antarctica
Type of Desert: Cold
Size: 14 million km²

Gibson Desert
Type of Desert: Hot
Size: 156,000 km²

Desert Habitats

*The edges of deserts are often covered with scattered **shrubs** and trees. The closer you move towards the centre of a desert, the more lifeless it gets.*

Hot Desert

The Dasht-e Loot desert in Iran was recorded by a NASA **satellite** as the hottest desert on Earth, with a surface **temperature** of 71 °C.

The edge of a desert will get more rain than the centre and it will often be **inhabited** by small trees, shrubs and cacti. The closer you get to the centre of the desert, the less life you will find. This is because the centre of a desert is often so dry or so cold that barely anything can live there. Some deserts, however, will have an oasis or two. These are large pools of water that form underground and push their way to the surface in the middle of deserts.

At the centre of hot deserts, only the toughest plants and animals can survive. Small shrubs grow in the shaded areas on sand dunes, where morning **dew** collects. This gives them just enough water to grow. At the centre of cold deserts, the ground is covered in snow, making it impossible for any plants to grow.

Sand Dunes, Sahara Desert

The plants and animals in deserts have needed to adapt to the small amount of rainfall. Many plants and animals survive in the desert by storing water. This means that they do not have to rely on regular rainfall for their water. Other animals reduce the amount of water they need simply by moving as little as possible.

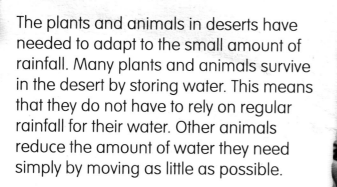

A polar bear emerging from its den.

There are many different types of cactus, all of which store water within their stem.

Desert animals have to survive extreme temperatures. One way they do this is by building a home under the sand or under the snow, called a burrow or den. This keeps them out of the burning heat in hot deserts and out of the freezing wind in cold deserts.

Arctic Desert

Desert Plants

Many plants that live in hot deserts can store water in their stems and use it later to make food.

The baobab tree stores water in its thick trunk for later use. Cacti also store water in their stems so that they can use it later. As well as this, cacti are covered in spikes to stop animals from eating their stems. Cactus plants mostly grow in America.

Cold deserts do not have trees because of the freezing temperatures. Trees, being large plants, often need a long period of good weather in order to grow properly. This is why many plants in cold deserts are only small, such as a cotton grass. Cotton grass grows quickly and can reproduce before it becomes too cold.

Cotton Grass

Many plants in cold deserts have dark leaves, which are better at absorbing small amounts of sunlight.

Baobab Tree

Not all plants play fair. The desert quandong, found in Australia, is a large shrub that grows a sweet fruit. While this shrub makes some food of its own, it also steals food from other plants. It does this by attaching its roots to the roots of other plants and then absorbing their **nutrients**. Plants that do this are said to be 'hemiparasitic'.

Desert plants grow lots of different types of unusual fruit. The prickly pear plant, found in America, grows a pear-like fruit with small spikes on it. The date palm tree, which grows in Africa, grows dark, juicy dates. These fruits are a very important source of food for the animals that live in the desert. Many animals also use fruit as a source of water.

The date palm fruit is often dried and sold as a tasty snack.

Prickly Pear Fruit

A date palm tree filled with dates.

Crawling Critters

Hot deserts are home to many different types of insect. Some have special adaptations that help them to survive in the heat of the desert.

Termites are found all around the world. Termites that live in the desert have adapted to be able to deal with the heat by building special nests. They build a huge tower from mud, called a termite mound, with a central 'chimney' and lots of small outer vents. During the night, when the air is cooler, the outer vents draw in cold air that flows around the nest.

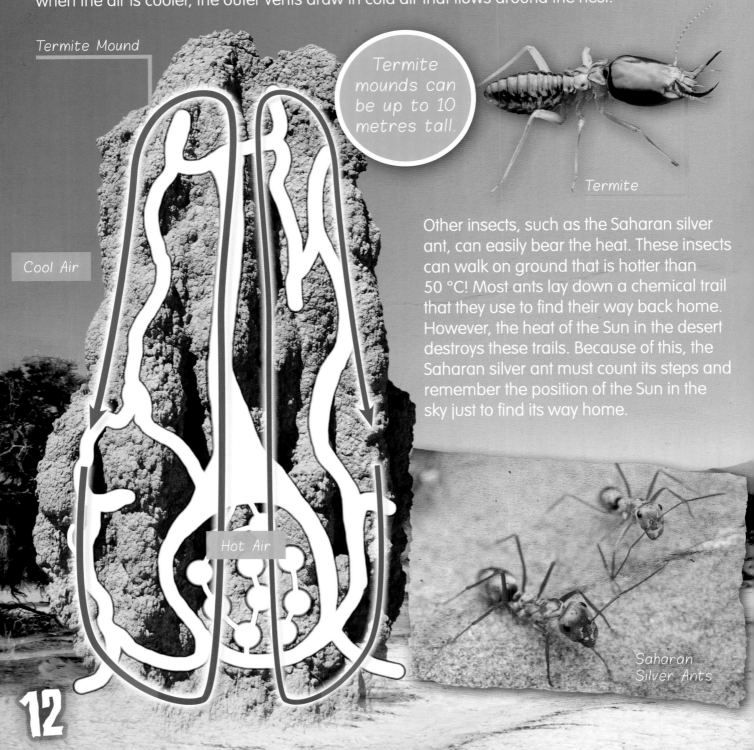

Termite Mound

Termite mounds can be up to 10 metres tall.

Cool Air

Hot Air

Termite

Other insects, such as the Saharan silver ant, can easily bear the heat. These insects can walk on ground that is hotter than 50 °C! Most ants lay down a chemical trail that they use to find their way back home. However, the heat of the Sun in the desert destroys these trails. Because of this, the Saharan silver ant must count its steps and remember the position of the Sun in the sky just to find its way home.

Saharan Silver Ants

Termites and ants are a tasty treat for the **arachnids** that live in the desert, such as the western desert tarantula. This large spider hunts by waiting for an insect to walk past its burrow and then quickly pouncing on it. By lying in wait for its prey, rather than searching the desert for it, the spider uses up less energy and therefore needs less water.

Western Desert Tarantula

Tarantula Hawk

The tarantula's most fearsome predator is the tarantula hawk. These insects **paralyse** tarantulas with a sting before laying their eggs inside the tarantula's body!

Deathstalker

One of the most famous critters in the desert is the scorpion. Many scorpions have a sting, but none have a sting as painful as that of the deathstalker scorpion. However, it's not the deathstalker's sting that makes it such a good desert survivor, but its ability to go without food for up to a year!

Digging Deep Underground

For many animals, the desert surface is just too hot during the day. To avoid the heat, some animals build underground burrows and stay in them until the heat of the day has passed.

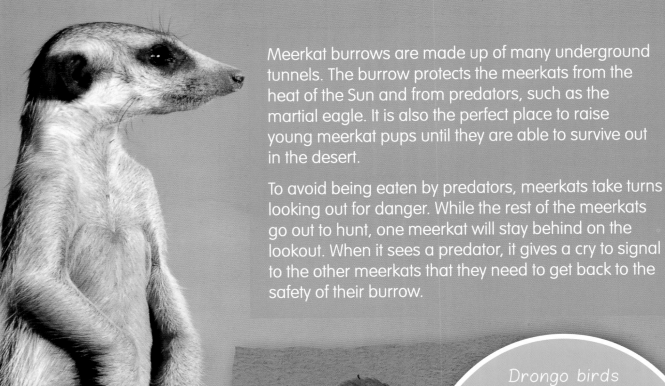

Meerkat burrows are made up of many underground tunnels. The burrow protects the meerkats from the heat of the Sun and from predators, such as the martial eagle. It is also the perfect place to raise young meerkat pups until they are able to survive out in the desert.

To avoid being eaten by predators, meerkats take turns looking out for danger. While the rest of the meerkats go out to hunt, one meerkat will stay behind on the lookout. When it sees a predator, it gives a cry to signal to the other meerkats that they need to get back to the safety of their burrow.

A meerkat in South Africa on the lookout for danger.

Drongo birds trick meerkats into running to their burrows by making the meerkat's sound for danger. As soon as the meerkats have hidden in their burrows, the drongo bird swoops down and eats their food.

The desert tortoise, unlike the meerkat, does not come out of its burrow very often and instead spends most of its life underground. To escape the heat of the Sun, the tortoise can dig up to two metres into the ground. This allows the tortoise to survive in deserts that have surface temperatures as hot as 60 °C.

The desert tortoise eats plants and fruit to get the water it needs.

In the Arctic, polar bears dig into the snow to make a den. The roof of the den protects the polar bear from freezing cold winds. These winds can reach speeds of up to 100 **km** per hour and can be as cold as -8 °C.

Polar bear cubs have to stay in their mother's den for three months after they are born because they cannot survive out in the cold.

A polar bear keeping out of the freezing winds.

True Survivors

Many desert animals have developed strange and amazing ways to survive.

The thorny dragon is a lizard that lives in Australian deserts and it has two very special **defences**. The lizard's body is covered in stiff spikes that make it very hard to eat, so most predators avoid it. It also has a fake head on the back of its neck that it will show when it is scared. This confuses the predator and causes it to attack the fake head instead of the lizard's real head.

Living at the edge of deserts in Africa are many giraffes. Giraffes have adapted to desert life by growing very long necks. This allows them to grab leaves from the tallest trees, which are too high for other **grazing animals** to get at.

False Head

Thorny Dragon

Giraffe

The giraffe's favourite tree is the thorny acacia. The giraffe has a long tongue that can avoid the thorns and grab the small leaves in between.

African elephants are often seen migrating through African deserts. Because of this, these elephants are also known as desert elephants. They are smaller than most other elephants and have become very good at finding water. They can find water that is trapped under the ground and will use their large feet and long trunks to dig down to it.

A family of African elephants digging for water.

The camel is perhaps the best desert survivor of them all. There are two main types of camel – dromedary camels, which have one hump, and Bactrian camels, which have two humps. The camels' humps are an adaptation that allows them to store fat. They use this store of fat when water is scarce, which means that they can go for up to seven months without needing to drink. This why humans often use them to cross deserts.

Dromedary Camel

Bactrian Camel

17

Big Hunters

*Every biome has special hunters that sit at the top of the **food chain**. These animals are called apex predators and they are rarely hunted by other creatures.*

The golden eagle sits at the top of its food chain and is the largest bird found in the desert. It can have a **wing-span** of up to two and a half metres. The golden eagle will only stay in the desert during the winter, when it is cooler. This bird has very good eyesight and can see prey from up to three kilometres away.

Golden Eagle

The longest desert snake is the desert kingsnake, which can grow up to two metres long. It kills by wrapping its body around its prey and squeezing. Snakes that kill in this way are known as constrictors. The desert kingsnake mostly eats small animals, such as mice and lizards.

Desert Kingsnake

African wild dogs, which live on the edges of deserts in Africa, have amazing hearing. Their ears act like big satellite dishes, allowing them to hear prey from very far away. They can also twist their ears, which allows them to pinpoint exactly where a sound is coming from.

African Wild Dog

One of the largest predators in the world is the lion. These mighty animals are found in many different habitats and biomes across Africa and some have even adapted to life in the desert. These lions mostly hunt gemsbok and other desert antelopes.

Lion

Gemsbok

19

Sand Dunes and Hamadas

Deserts are known for their rolling sand dunes and dry hamadas. Sand dunes are hills of sand that can grow to enormous sizes, while hamadas are hard, rocky areas where all the sand has been blown away.

Because the sand on the sand dunes is easily blown around, the hills often change shape and move around, making it difficult for plants to take root. However, some plants, such as the saxaul, manage to find a way.

On most mornings in the Namib deserts, a thick fog rolls over the sand dunes. This is an important opportunity for fogstand beetles to collect water. These beetles rush to the tops of the sand dunes and stand with their heads facing the ground. The water in the fog then collects in little droplets on the beetles' bodies.

Fogstand Beetle

Saxaul

The sand that makes up sand dunes moves around easily and is often very soft, which makes it hard to walk across. Because of this, the fringe-toed lizard in America has adapted special scales on its feet that help it to walk around. The lizard also has thick eyelids and flaps around its nose that it uses to stop sand from getting into its body.

Fringe-Toed Lizard

Sand cats, despite their name, mostly live in hamadas where there is very little sand. They have thick fur that protects their feet from the scorching hot ground. They also have large ears that help them to stay cool. Hot blood is pumped from their body to their ears where it is cooled by the wind.

Sand Cat

A hamada in Israel.

Extreme Landscapes

Oases

An oasis is a body of water in the middle of a desert. Oases form in areas that are surrounded by large hills. This is because water from the hills will flow underground to a single point in the middle of the desert. Eventually, enough water builds up underground that it pushes its way to the surface, forming an oasis.

Oases are the perfect place for migrating animals to stop and have a drink. Because oases are so far away from other plants and bodies of water, they are often home to plants and animals that cannot be found anywhere else in the world. Kufra honeybees, for example, have been separated from other honeybees around the world for over 5,000 years. This has kept the bees safe from deadly parasites that have affected other bee species.

Honeybees

The village of Huacachina in Peru is built around an oasis.

Salt Pans

Salt pans, also called salt flats, are large areas of white desert land. They are covered in a thick, crusty layer of salt, which is what gives them their white colour. This salt, however, stops any plants from growing, making it impossible for animals to survive in these deserts. Salt pans form when sea water becomes cut off from the rest of the ocean and evaporates in the sunlight. The salt in the ocean water gets left behind on the ground.

The salt flats in America are so large that many people use them for driving the fastest cars in the world, which need lots of space.

Ice Sheets

An ice sheet is an area of land that is covered in ice and is at least 50,000 km² in size. That's more than twice the size of Wales. Nothing can grow or survive on an ice sheet because it is too cold.

The largest ice sheet is in Antarctica and it is 600 times larger than Wales.

Antarctica

23

Sahara

The largest hot desert in the world is the Sahara. It covers over nine million square kilometres, crosses eleven countries and stretches all the way from Africa's east coast to its west coast. This desert is so large that when people talk about it, they often break it up into seven smaller areas. These areas are called Western Sahara, the Hoggar Mountains, the Tibesti Mountains, the Aïr Mountains, the Ténéré desert region and the Libyan Desert.

The Sahara can be as hot as 40 °C and the desert's surface can reach temperatures as high as 80 °C. The desert gets as little as eight centimetres of rainfall a year, whereas a country like Scotland can receive over 150 centimetres of rainfall a year.

West Coast

Sahara

East Coast

Under such dry conditions, dust storms can form. These storms are made up of huge clouds of dust that drift across many countries.

Because the Sahara is so dry during the summer, many of the animals that live there, such as camels and elephants, **migrate** to cooler areas. Some plants in the Sahara also become dormant during the summer. This means that they slow down or stop growing, which helps them to survive the dry summer season.

This family of elephants are migrating to avoid the summer heat.

Global warming is causing deserts to become even hotter and drier than normal. The dry conditions have led to many wildfires. These wildfires do happen naturally but, because of global warming, they have been happening more often. When they happen too often, plants get destroyed and there is little food for grazing animals to eat.

A desert after a wildfire.

25

Antarctica

Antarctica is the largest cold desert in the world at 14 million km² in size. This makes it the largest desert in the world. Even though about 98% of the area is covered in ice, hundreds of species still manage to live there.

Antarctica gets, at most, 20 centimetres of rain a year. However, it is not the lack of rain that makes Antarctica so difficult to survive in. It's the cold temperatures. Antarctica has an average yearly temperature of around -49 °C – the average freezer only goes as low as -18 °C.

Antarctica

Most of the animals in Antarctica live near the coast and most rely on food in the sea, where it's warmer. Many species of bird only stay in Antarctica during the summer and will migrate during the winter but emperor penguins are able to withstand the harsh climate all year round. They have adapted to be able to reproduce during the coldest months in Antarctica, when fewer predators are around to prey on their young.

A waddle of Emperor Penguins with their chicks.

A group of emperor penguins is called a waddle.

Over the past few years, the ice in Antarctica has begun to melt more and more quickly due to global warming. This melting ice has a terrible effect on the rest of the world. When the ice melts, it adds more water into the ocean and causes sea levels to rise. Rising sea levels will cause beaches and other habitats to become flooded. On top of this, the animals in Antarctica lose their hunting grounds as the ice melts away.

Flood in Kuttanad, India

Saving the Deserts

GLOBAL WARMING

The greatest threat to the world's deserts is the Earth's rising temperature. As the planet gets warmer, the hot deserts get even drier and the cold deserts begin to melt. This will result in more wildfires and serious flooding.

The planet is warming due to greenhouse gases, such as carbon dioxide, building up in Earth's **atmosphere**. Carbon dioxide is supposed to be in the atmosphere, but too much of it stops the Sun's heat from escaping the Earth. Reducing the amount of carbon dioxide in the air is the best way to stop global warming.

Car exhaust fumes release a lot of carbon dioxide into the atmosphere.

One of the best ways to reduce the amount of carbon dioxide in the atmosphere is to grow more plants. Plants absorb carbon dioxide and turn it into oxygen. So, by planting trees or growing your own vegetables, you can help to reduce carbon dioxide levels and the effects of global warming.

Many vehicles, such as cars, trains and planes, give off a lot of carbon dioxide. The more we use these vehicles, the more carbon dioxide is released into the air, meaning that we should try to walk and cycle as much as we can. For long journeys, we should try to take the bus or another form of public transport so that there are fewer vehicles on the road.

Quick Quiz and Useful Links

Quick Quiz

On average, how much rainfall does a hot desert get each year?

How do meerkats avoid predators?

What adaptation helps camels to survive in the desert?

What do we call the sandy hills in deserts?

What is the name of the largest hot desert?

What is the main cause of global warming?

Useful Links

Discover more about animals and their habitats by visiting
www.ngkids.co.uk

Find loads of desert wildlife videos and images at
www.bbc.co.uk/nature/habitats/Deserts_and_xeric_shrublands

Learn more about deserts and animals under threat at
www.wwf.org.uk

Find out how you can help stop global warming at
climatekids.nasa.gov/menu/big-questions

Glossary

°C	the symbol for degrees Celsius, the metric measurement of temperature
adapted	changed over time to suit different conditions
artificial	not natural
atmosphere	the mixture of gases that make up the air and surround the Earth
climate	the common weather in a certain place
dew	tiny drops of water that form on cool surfaces at night
evaporate	turn from a liquid into a gas or vapour
food chain	a way of showing what each animal in a habitat eats – food chains show how the organisms in a habitat are all connected
grazing animals	animals that eat lots of plants to get their nutrients
inhabited	lived in or occupied by
km	kilometres
migrate	move from one place to another based on seasonal changes
nutrients	natural substances that are needed for animals and plants to grow
paralyse	cause to be unable to move
predators	animals that hunt other animals for food
reproduce	to have young through the act of mating
satellite	a machine in space that travels around a planet, taking photographs and collecting and transmitting information
sea level	the level of the sea's surface, which is often used as a base level to measure height by
shrubs	woody plants and bushes
temperature	how hot something is
wingspan	the distance between the tips of a bird's wings

Index